Student Activity Guide for

Goals for Living

Managing Your Resources

by

Nancy Wehlage
Portage, Wisconsin

Mary Larson-Kennedy, CFCS
Delavan, Wisconsin

Publisher
The Goodheart-Willcox Company, Inc.
Tinley Park, Illinois
www.g-w.com

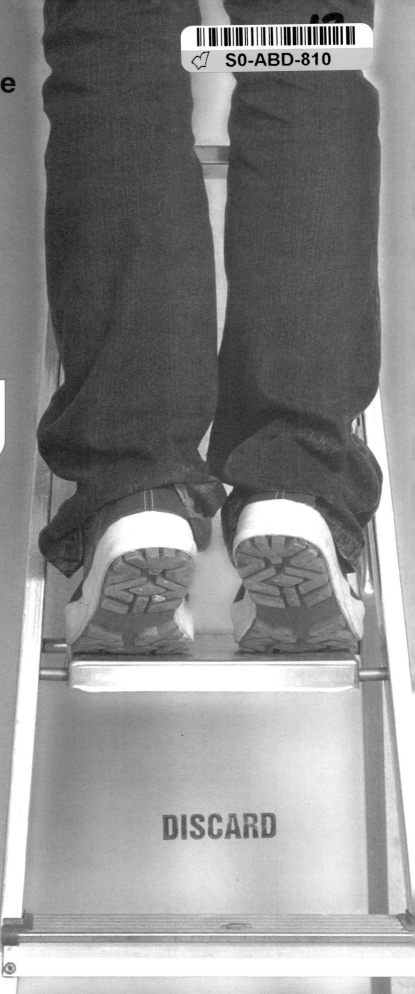

DISCARD

S0-ABD-810

Introduction

This activity guide is designed for use with the text, **_Goals for Living: Managing Your Resources._** Doing the activities will help you to review and recall concepts presented in the text. These activities will also help you to apply concepts in management to your daily life. You will learn how to manage your resources to reach your goals.

The activities in this guide are divided into chapters that correspond to chapters in the text. Read the text first and then try to complete the activities without looking back at the text. You should have the information needed to complete each activity. When you have completed an activity, refer to the text to check your answers and complete any questions you could not answer.

This guide contains several kinds of activities. Some of them have "right" answers. These activities can be used to help you review for tests and quizzes. Other activities ask for opinions, evaluations, and conclusions that cannot be judged as "right" or "wrong." These activities are designed to encourage you to consider alternatives, evaluate situations thoughtfully, and apply information in the text to your own life.

Cover source: Getty Images

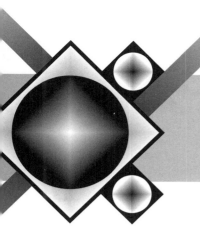

Contents

Decision Making in Your Daily Life

Daily Decision Making

Activity A

Chapter 1

Name _____

Date _____ Period _____

You are a manager. You make many decisions each day that can help you reach your goals. Think about your activities of the last few days. Then write an example of a decision you have made related to each area of living listed below.

1. A decision involving your family: _____

_____

_____

_____

2. A decision involving your relationships with others: _____

_____

_____

_____

3. A decision involving your health: _____

_____

_____

_____

4. A decision involving food: _____

_____

_____

_____

5. A decision involving clothing: _____

_____

_____

_____

6. A decision involving you as a consumer: _____

_____

_____

_____

(Continued)

Refer to the six examples on the previous page and fill in the chart with values, goals, and resources that are related to each decision.

	Values	Goals	Resources
1.			
2.			
3.			
4.			
5.			
6.			

Decisions, Decisions, Decisions!

Activity B

Chapter 1

Name _____

Date _____ **Period** _____

The chart below lists several stages in life. Fill in the chart with three decisions typically made in each stage.

Stage in Life	Decisions Typically Made
Teenager	1. _____ _____ 2. _____ _____ 3. _____ _____
Young Adult	1. _____ _____ 2. _____ _____ 3. _____ _____
Middle-Age Adult	1. _____ _____ 2. _____ _____ 3. _____ _____
Senior Citizen	1. _____ _____ 2. _____ _____ 3. _____ _____

(Continued)

The chart below lists various roles in life. Fill in the chart with examples of two decisions typically made in each role.

Role in Life	Decisions Typically Made
Individual	1. _____ _____ 2. _____ _____
Family Member	1. _____ _____ 2. _____ _____
Parent	1. _____ _____ 2. _____ _____
Employee	1. _____ _____ 2. _____ _____
Community Member	1. _____ _____ 2. _____ _____

Recognizing Your Resources

Name _____

Date _____ Period _____

Many resources are available to you or can be developed to help you reach your goals. For each goal below, list at least three resources that could help you reach that goal.

Goal	Resources to Help Me Reach the Goal
To get a good part-time job while still in school	
To be a good friend to others	
To improve my grades in school	
To be a healthy person	
To get a college education	
To buy a car	
To be a good cook	
To be a good parent	
To own my own home	
To be prepared for the later years of life	

Skills in Solving Problems

Name _____

Date _____ Period _____

Think of a problem you would like to solve. Following the steps of the decision-making process, try to solve the problem.

State the problem as a goal:

_____

_____

List the alternatives and consequences of each alternative:

_____

_____

_____

_____

_____

_____

Choose the best alternative:

_____

_____

_____

_____

State the outcome of the decision:

_____

_____

Evaluate the decision and the process:

_____

_____

_____

_____

_____

_____

Your Values, Goals, and Standards

Value Identification

Activity A

Chapter 2

Name _____

Date _____ **Period** _____

List and describe the three main categories of higher values. Give at least two examples of each type of value.

1. _____ : _____

_____

_____

Examples: _____

2. _____ : _____

_____

_____

Examples: _____

3. _____ : _____

_____

_____

Examples: _____

Indicate which category of higher value relates to each of the following.

1. A beautiful sunset _____

2. Returning a billfold to its owner _____

3. Rest _____

4. A smoothly running car _____

5. Voting in an election _____

6. Recognition _____

7. Self-worth _____

8. Admitting that you lied _____

9. Your favorite dessert _____

10. Obeying the speed limit _____

11. Food _____

12. The skill of an athlete_____

Values and Behavior

Name _____

Date _____ Period _____

Behaviors are a reflection of a person's values. List two different values in the blanks below. Beneath each value, list three behaviors (actions, statements, activities) that indicate that value.

1. Value:_____

    A. _____

    B. _____

    C. _____

2. Value:_____

    A. _____

    B. _____

    C. _____

List four activities in which you have recently participated or actions you have taken. Following each activity, list the value or values that motivated your action.

Activity or Action	Value(s)
1. _____	_____
2. _____	_____
3. _____	_____
4. _____	_____

List three statements that could indicate a person's values. Following each statement, write the value indicated. For example, the statement "It makes me mad when he is late" shows that promptness is a value.

Statement	Value(s)
1. _____	_____
_____	_____
2. _____	_____
_____	_____
3. _____	_____
_____	_____

Values and Value Sources

Activity C

Chapter 2

Name _____

Date _____ Period _____

List three higher-level values in the left column. In the right column, list three instrumental values that lead to higher-level value. Example: A higher-level value is happiness. Instrumental values that might lead to happiness are my dog, going on a vacation, and winning a tennis match.

Higher-Level Values   Instrumental Values

1. _____   A. _____

                                                            B. _____

                                                            C. _____

2. _____   A. _____

                                                            B. _____

                                                            C. _____

3. _____   A. _____

                                                            B. _____

                                                            C. _____

Children learn values from models. List four actions a parent might take that would influence a child's values.

1. _____

2. _____

3. _____

4. _____

List two actions a teenager might take that would influence a younger brother or sister's values.

1. _____

2. _____

Goals and Standards

Name _____

Date _____ Period _____

Complete the charts below with information relating to short- and long-term goals. First, list the goal. Then list the values on which that goal is based. Finally, describe the standards you could use to judge whether that goal has been reached.

Short-Term Goals	Value(s)	Standards
Examples: A. To lose five pounds in two months B. To pass the math test	Looking nice Good grades	Five pounds less on the scale Score above passing
1.		
2.		
3.		

Long-Term Goals	Value(s)	Standards
1.		
2.		
3.		

Managing Your Resources

Identifying Resources

Name _____

Date _____ Period _____

Complete the outline on types of resources by placing the following terms where they belong.

capabilities, talents, skills
stores
car
time
friends
money and purchasing
  power
clothing

good mental health
athletic ability
other persons
wages
personal qualities
material possessions
credit
house

good physical health
a beautiful singing
  voice
police protection
natural resources
skill in writing
community resources
parents

I. Human resources

A. _____

B. _____

   1. Pleasant personality

   2. _____

   3. _____

C. _____

   1. _____

   2. _____

   3. _____

D. _____

   1. Family

   2. _____

   3. _____

(Continued)

Name _____

II. Nonhuman resources

   A. _____

      1. _____

      2. _____

      3. _____

   B. _____

      1. Allowance

      2. _____

      3. _____

   C. _____

      1. Schools

      2. _____

      3. _____

      4. _____

Resources to Manage

Name _____

Date _____ Period _____

List six resources you have used followed by a brief description of the activity in which those resources were used. Then indicate the type of resource. Refer to the outline in Activity A if necessary.

Resources	Activity	Type of Resource
Examples: Skill in gardening Electric mixer	Growing various vegetables Baking cookies	Human—skill Nonhuman—possession
1.		
2.		
3.		
4.		
5.		
6.		

Write an example of an action you might take to conserve each of the resources listed.

Resource	Action to Conserve Resource
Examples: Gasoline	In order to save gas, Heidi decides to walk four blocks to the grocery store instead of driving.
1. Money	
2. Time	
3. Water	
4. Energy	

Using the Management Process

Name _____

Date _____ Period _____

Today is Saturday, and Scott Sanborn's parents have been called out of town unexpectedly due to the illness of a friend. Scott, who works at a local restaurant on the weekends, has been asked to help his parents while they are gone. Scott's mother usually does her grocery shopping on Saturday. She has left her grocery list for Scott so he can do the shopping. Scott's father is expecting a c.o.d. (cash on delivery) package in the mail and would like Scott to be home when it arrives.

Describe how Scott could use the management process to manage the day's activities. Use these facts to help you:

1. Scott is scheduled to work the morning shift from 6:00 a.m. to 8:00 a.m. and the afternoon shift from noon to 6:00 p.m.
2. The mail is usually delivered between 11:00 a.m. and 11:30 a.m.
3. Scott has a car to use.
4. The grocery store and the restaurant are both about a five minute drive from Scott's home.
5. Scott can eat breakfast at work but needs to eat lunch at home.
6. The grocery store opens at 8:00 a.m.
7. The grocery list contains some items that will need to be refrigerated.

Planning: Describe the factors you need to consider before developing a plan for Scott. Then write out a good plan.

_____

_____

_____

_____

_____

_____

_____

Implementing and Controlling: List some events that could force Scott to change his plan if they occur. How could Scott show flexibility in controlling his plan?

_____

_____

_____

_____

_____

_____

Evaluating: Describe how Scott will know if his plan is successful.

_____

_____

_____

_____

_____

_____

Managing Time and Energy

Activity D   **Name** _____

Chapter 3   **Date** _____ **Period** _____

Choose an activity you do repeatedly during the week but feel you could do more efficiently. Break the activity down into details of what must be done. Analyze the activity and develop a new procedure that would improve your use of time and energy.

Activity:_____

Steps you presently take to complete the activity:

_____

_____

_____

_____

_____

_____

_____

_____

Analyze the steps mentioned. List three questions that were suggested in the textbook for simplifying an activity.

1. _____

_____

2. _____

_____

3. _____

_____

Suggest a new method of completing the activity. _____

_____

_____

_____

_____

List the changes you made and explain why you made them._____

_____

_____

_____

_____

Technology as a Resource

Technology Today

Name _____

Date _____ Period _____

In the left column, list examples of technology in your home or workplace. In the right column, describe how each item is helpful to your daily living.

Example of Technology	How It Is Helpful
1.	
2.	
3.	
4.	

(Continued)

Name _____

Example of Technology	How It Is Helpful
5.	
6.	
7.	
8.	

Benefits and Concerns of Technology

Name _____

Date _____ Period _____

Although people benefit from technology, there are also important concerns regarding some of the undesirable effects. In the chart below, list various benefits and concerns related to the specific technology described.

Technology	Benefits	Concerns
Automated manufacturing through robotics		
Computers and computer software		
The Internet		
Electronic banking and bill paying		
Advances in the area of agriculture		
Biotechnology		

Technology and the Future

Name _____

Date _____ Period _____

Look through current magazines and newspapers to find an article about a technological innovation planned for the future. In the space provided, describe this innovation and possible benefits and concerns.

Describe the technological innovation: _____

_____

_____

_____

_____

_____

_____

_____

_____

_____

_____

_____

_____

_____

_____

_____

_____

_____

How will this new technology benefit society? _____

_____

_____

_____

_____

_____

What concerns are related to this technological innovation? _____

_____

_____

Understanding Development

Hereditary and Environmental Influences

Activity A

Chapter 5

Name _____

Date _____ **Period** _____

Ask someone who knows you well, such as a family member or a close friend, to write 10 sentences that describe something about you. These sentences might describe how you look, how you feel, how you act, or what you do. Choose five of the 10 sentences and write them in the spaces below. Below each sentence, explain whether you think the characteristics described are influenced by heredity or the environment.

1. _____
   _____
   _____

2. _____
   _____
   _____
   _____

3. _____
   _____
   _____
   _____

4. _____
   _____
   _____
   _____

5. _____
   _____
   _____

Which of the above characteristics would you like to change? What could you do to make this change?

_____
_____
_____
_____
_____

Patterns of Development

Name _____

Date _____ Period _____

No two people mature at the same rate. For each area of development listed below, think of two teenagers you know who are at different levels of maturity. Then fill in the information requested.

Physical Development: Write adjectives that describe two teenagers the same age who differ physically.

Person #1	Person #2

Social Development: Write adjectives that describe two teenagers who differ greatly in relation to social maturity.

Person #1	Person #2

Emotional Development: Write descriptions of two teenagers who differ greatly in relation to emotional maturity.

Person #1	Person #2

Intellectual Development: Describe instances leading you to believe two teenagers differ greatly in relation to intellectual development.

Person #1	Person #2

Self-Concept

Name _____

Date _____ Period _____

Your self-concept includes how you see yourself with respect to your personal self, social self, ideal self, and extended self. Indicate which aspect of self-concept is being illustrated in each example by putting the appropriate letter in the blank.

_____ 1. Female.

_____ 2. A good sport.

_____ 3. Actions imitating someone you admire.

_____ 4. Skinny.

_____ 5. A special group in which you are very active.

_____ 6. Sociable.

_____ 7. Happy.

_____ 8. Image of who you would like to be.

_____ 9. Tall.

_____ 10. Serious.

_____ 11. Disorganized.

_____ 12. Your family.

_____ 13. Handsome.

_____ 14. Able to make friends easily.

_____ 15. Moody.

_____ 16. Male.

_____ 17. At ease in conversations.

_____ 18. Responsible.

_____ 19. Image of someone you admire.

_____ 20. Pretty.

_____ 21. Your special group of friends.

_____ 22. Immature.

_____ 23. Your team.

_____ 24. Physically fit.

_____ 25. Prefer to be alone.

A. personal self

B. social self

C. ideal self

D. extended self

Formation of the Self-Concept

Activity D   **Name** _____

Chapter 5   **Date** _____ **Period** _____

Briefly explain how each of the following situations might affect the person's self-concept.

1. Three-month-old Liam is a lucky baby. His parents work hard to provide a caring environment in which Liam's everyday world is a healthy and happy one.

   _____

   _____

2. Jimmy, a kindergartener, is struggling with learning numbers and letters. Annoyed by this, his father asks, "What's wrong with you, Jimmy? Why can't you learn numbers and letters like most of the other kids?"

   _____

   _____

3. Terrence, a high school student, has not yet experienced his adolescent growth spurt. His voice is high, and his cheeks are smooth and hairless. He is much shorter than many of his friends.

   _____

   _____

4. Sharon is the only student in her class who received a perfect score on the final exam.

   _____

   _____

5. Cheryl was fired from her job at a fast-food restaurant after she was late for work three days in a row.

   _____

   _____

6. As 45-year-old Walter sat in the stands, he watched his son, Earl, lead the football team to a victory.

   _____

   _____

7. At 50 years of age, Joyce tried downhill skiing for the first time. After several lessons, she was thoroughly enjoying this new challenge.

   _____

   _____

8. Martha, whose health is failing, has just moved from her apartment into a nursing home.

   _____

   _____

Development During the Early Years

Sequence of Development

Name _____

Date _____ Period _____

Find four pictures in magazines or actual photos that illustrate sequence in development in one of the four areas of development: physical, social, emotional, or intellectual. Place the photos in their proper order. Then write a brief explanation below each photo telling what that photo illustrates related to that area of development.

Area of Development: _____

1.

Explanation: _____

_____

_____

(Continued)

2.

Explanation: _____

_____

_____

3.

Explanation: _____

_____

_____

4.

Explanation: _____

_____

_____

Development of Children

Activity B Name _____

Chapter 6 Date _____ Period _____

Below are listed phrases that describe stages children go through in their physical, social, emotional, and intellectual development. Read each phrase and decide if it describes the development of infants and toddlers, preschool children, or school-age children. Then write the correct letter in the blank.

A. infants and toddlers

B. preschool children

C. school-age children

Physical Development

_____ 1. Eye-hand coordination begins to develop.

_____ 2. The first permanent molars are emerging.

_____ 3. More individual variations in growth.

_____ 4. Enjoy most athletic activities.

_____ 5. Run and climb.

_____ 6. Teeth begin to erupt.

_____ 7. Girls show signs of approaching adolescence.

_____ 8. Need some help dressing.

_____ 9. Show hand preference.

_____ 10. Learn bowel and bladder control.

_____ 11. Walk and run with good balance.

_____ 12. Enjoy physical games and sports.

Physical Development

_____ 13. Imaginary playmates are common.

_____ 14. Like to talk a lot.

_____ 15. Seek attention of others.

_____ 16. Often fight with siblings.

_____ 17. More accepting and sensitive to needs of others.

_____ 18. Play next to other children, but not with them cooperatively.

_____ 19. Friends become very important.

_____ 20. Begin to play in a cooperative way.

(Continued)

_____ 21. Often involved in clubs and organized groups.

_____ 22. Afraid of strangers.

_____ 23. Get along better with older siblings than with younger siblings.

_____ 24. Imitate parents' work.

_____ 25. Learn social skills through trial and error with friends.

Emotional Development

_____ 26. Strong emotional attachment to mother.

_____ 27. More controlled about expressing themselves.

_____ 28. Demand a lot of parental attention.

_____ 29. Compulsive behaviors like stuttering and thumbsucking are normal.

_____ 30. Have normal fears of falling and loud noises.

_____ 31. Frightening dreams are frequent.

_____ 32. Begin to accept responsibility for their behavior.

_____ 33. A happy, less tearful stage.

Intellectual Development

_____ 34. Use language fluently.

_____ 35. Learn to count and print.

_____ 36. May repeat familiar words.

_____ 37. Interested in putting things together.

_____ 38. Ethical sense is developing.

_____ 39. Are very curious.

_____ 40. Rapid language development.

_____ 41. Enjoyment of reading may increase.

_____ 42. Mathematical skills develop.

_____ 43. Recognize sounds and familiar voices.

_____ 44. Understand simple commands.

_____ 45. Can form abstract ideas.

Play and Intellectual Development

Activity C

Chapter 6

Name _____

Date _____ Period _____

Young children acquire much of their knowledge through play. Give examples that show how children can learn from each of the following experiences.

Watching others play: _____

_____

_____

_____

_____

_____

_____

Symbolic play: _____

_____

_____

_____

_____

_____

_____

Pretend play: _____

_____

_____

_____

_____

_____

_____

Learning through their senses: _____

_____

_____

_____

_____

_____

The Developing Self-Concept

Name _____

Date _____ Period _____

Read the following situations and explain how each experience might affect a child's developing self-concept. Indicate why you think the experience would have that effect.

1. Susie, age three, throws her baby brother's pacifier in the garbage. Her mother spanks her and makes her go to her room.

   _____

   _____

   _____

2. Jamal's model airplane, which he put together completely by himself, wins first place in the model show at school.

   _____

   _____

   _____

3. Lakeisha's father says, "Lakeisha, please go outside and play. Your mother, brother and I are discussing a family matter that you wouldn't understand."

   _____

   _____

   _____

4. Eight-year-old Gary went to see his favorite baseball team play. While he was at the game, Gary met his favorite player and had him sign his baseball.

   _____

   _____

   _____

5. Michelle showed her painting of a boat to the class, and many of her classmates snickered and laughed.

   _____

   _____

   _____

6. Michelle's teacher said, "That is an unusual boat. It would be fun to see a real one like that. You have used very pretty colors in your painting."

   _____

   _____

   _____

7. When telling his four-year-old son good night, Mr. Benson said, "This has been such a special day for me, Tommy. You and I had so much fun together—the trip to the zoo, the walk in the park, and the visit to the ice cream shop. I enjoyed spending the day with you."

   _____

   _____

   _____

Developmental Tasks of Childhood

Developmental Tasks of Infants and Toddlers

Activity A

Chapter 7

Name _____

Date _____ **Period** _____

List the six developmental tasks for infants and toddlers discussed in the text. Then name two things a parent or someone else close to a child could do to encourage the child to accomplish each task.

1. Task: _____

   _____

   A. _____

   _____

   B. _____

   _____

2. Task: _____

   _____

   A. _____

   _____

   B. _____

   _____

3. Task: _____

   _____

   A. _____

   _____

   B. _____

   _____

4. Task: _____

   _____

   A. _____

   _____

   B. _____

(Continued)

Name _____

5. Task: _____

_____

  A. _____

_____

  B. _____

_____

6. Task: _____

_____

  A. _____

_____

  B. _____

_____

Developmental Tasks of Preschool Children

Activity B Name _____

Chapter 7 Date _____ Period _____

Each of the statements below indicates that a preschool child has achieved a particular developmental task. Read each statement and then write the letter of the appropriate developmental task in the blank. Each letter will be used three times.

Developmental Tasks

    A. developing healthy daily routines

    B. developing physical skills

    C. learning through expanded experiences and more effective communication

    D. learning to express feelings and control actions

    E. being an active member of the family

    F. strengthening self-concept while becoming more independent

_____ 1. David helps his older sister put the leaves she has raked into garbage bags.

_____ 2. Eric rides his tricycle for hours each day.

_____ 3. Christy tells her brother she is sorry for breaking his truck.

_____ 4. Garrett learned a fun new game at his friend's birthday party and taught it to his sister.

_____ 5. Latoya got a puzzle for her birthday and has been playing with it ever since.

_____ 6. When it is nearly bedtime, Michael says he is sleepy and puts on his pajamas.

_____ 7. James goes into the bathroom to brush his teeth after every meal.

_____ 8. Renardo hangs his jacket on the hook in his room whenever he comes home.

_____ 9. Andy tells his mommy he loves her.

_____ 10. Julie washes her hands before every meal.

_____ 11. Jamie helps her father do carpentry work by handing him nails as he needs them.

_____ 12. Scott loves to go to the park to run around and play on the swings.

_____ 13. Karen has countless adventures with her pretend friend, Susie.

_____ 14. Rob makes friends easily at his new preschool.

_____ 15. Madeline works with her mother and brother to decorate Christmas cookies, a yearly tradition.

_____ 16. Willie recently got a new puppy, and they have become inseparable.

_____ 17. Although Paul is angry with his brother, he resists the urge to hit him or throw toys.

_____ 18. Sandra insists on putting on her winter coat and snow boots without her mother's help.

Developmental Tasks of School-Age Children

Activity C

Chapter 7

Name _____

Date _____ **Period** _____

Name the developmental tasks of school-age children discussed in the text. For each task, list examples of two behaviors that would show a child has achieved that task.

1. Task: _____

   A. _____

   _____

   B. _____

   _____

2. Task: _____

   A. _____

   _____

   B. _____

   _____

3. Task: _____

   A. _____

   _____

   B. _____

   _____

4. Task: _____

   A. _____

   _____

   B. _____

   _____

5. Task: _____

   A. _____

   _____

   B. _____

   _____

6. Task: _____

   A. _____

   _____

   B. _____

   _____

Developmental Tasks from Adolescence Throughout Life

Developmental Tasks

Activity A

Chapter 8

Name _____

Date _____ Period _____

Suppose a friend wants to know how he or she is doing in achieving the developmental tasks of adolescence. For each task listed below, write three questions that might help your friend make this analysis.

Developmental Task: To accept and manage your changing body

1. _____
   _____
2. _____
   _____
3. _____
   _____

Developmental Task: To be involved in a variety of social experiences

1. _____
   _____
2. _____
   _____
3. _____
   _____

Developmental Task: To assume more responsibility while moving toward greater independence

1. _____
   _____
2. _____
   _____
3. _____

(Continued)

Name _____

Developmental Task: To develop personal resources helpful in reaching future goals

1. _____

_____

2. _____

_____

3. _____

_____

Developmental Task: To continue to develop a healthy self-concept

1. _____

_____

2. _____

_____

3. _____

_____

Developmental Tasks of the Young Adult

Activity B   **Name** _____

Chapter 8   **Date** _____ **Period** _____

Below are listed some of the developmental tasks of young adults. Indicate what you can do now to make it easier to achieve these developmental tasks as a young adult.

1. To prepare for and become successfully involved in a career _____

_____

_____

_____

_____

2. To expand social relationships and assume social responsibilities _____

_____

_____

_____

_____

3. To exercise management skills related to daily living _____

_____

_____

_____

_____

4. To continue self-enriching pursuits _____

_____

_____

_____

_____

5. To assess readiness for marriage_____

_____

_____

_____

_____

6. To assess readiness for parenthood _____

_____

_____

_____

_____

Developmental Tasks of Middle-Age Adults

Activity C

Chapter 8

Name _____

Date _____ Period _____

Consider the developmental tasks of middle-age people. Suggest healthy ways and ideas to meet the needs of this stage. You may want to get suggestions from parents, friends, and even grandparents who are middle aged. What have they done to meet their developmental needs?

1. To continue self-enriching vocational and avocational pursuits _____

_____

_____

_____

_____

2. To adjust to physiological changes _____

_____

_____

_____

_____

3. To continue family responsibilities _____

_____

_____

_____

_____

4. To further the growth of marital relationship _____

_____

_____

_____

_____

5. To manage daily living _____

_____

_____

_____

_____

6. To prepare for later years _____

_____

_____

_____

_____

Developmental Tasks of Late Adulthood

Activity D

Chapter 8

Name _____

Date _____ Period _____

Think of older adults in their later adulthood years. In what ways have they managed the developmental tasks of later adulthood? List the ways below. If they haven't managed well, what are some positive suggestions that might help.

1. To care for oneself physically _____

_____

_____

_____

_____

2. To continue self-enriching pursuits _____

_____

_____

_____

_____

3. To maintain family contacts and responsibilities _____

_____

_____

_____

_____

4. To adjust to retirement changes in income and living arrangements _____

_____

_____

_____

_____

5. To adapt positively to the certainty of death _____

_____

_____

_____

_____

Successful Relationships

Describing Successful Relationships

Activity A

Chapter 9

Name _____

Date _____ Period _____

Show that you understand the importance of respect, trust, responsibility, and openness by developing a situation to fit each of the following descriptions.

1. Trust being shown in a parent-child relationship _____

_____

_____

_____

_____

_____

2. Responsibility being shown in a relationship between a husband and wife _____

_____

_____

_____

_____

_____

3. Respect being shown between two teenage friends _____

_____

_____

_____

_____

_____

4. Openness being shown between a couple who are dating _____

_____

_____

_____

_____

_____

(Continued)

5. Trust being shown in a relationship between two teenage friends _____

_____

_____

_____

_____

6. Openness being shown between a parent and child _____

_____

_____

_____

_____

7. Respect being shown between a parent and child _____

_____

_____

_____

_____

8. Openness being shown between a husband and wife _____

_____

_____

_____

_____

The Basis of Good Relationships

Name _____

Date _____ Period _____

Read each of the following statements. Circle *T* if the statement is true. Circle *F* if the statement is false. If a statement is false, correct it in the space provided.

T   F   1. Respecting a person is the same as liking that person. _____

_____

_____

_____

T   F   2. If a special relationship is to exist between you and another person, mutual respect is necessary. _____

_____

_____

_____

T   F   3. Stereotyping usually indicates a type of respect for a person. _____

_____

_____

_____

T   F   4. Although trust develops quickly, it takes time to destroy. _____

_____

_____

_____

T   F   5. All relationships carry with them certain assumed responsibilities. _____

_____

_____

_____

T   F   6. There is no risk involved in being open. _____

_____

_____

T   F   7. Acceptance means always agreeing with the other person. _____

_____

_____

_____

T   F   8. People who are accepting try to understand your feelings without judging whether you are right or wrong. _____

_____

_____

_____

Learning from Relationships

Name _____

Date _____ Period _____

Describe a situation that illustrates each of the following statements.

Example: During the middle and late adult years, relationships outside the family become more meaningful.	Mr. Pablos and Mr. Harris meet daily and walk downtown to have a cup of coffee and visit. Both elderly men are widowers. Their friendship is important to them. They each have someone else who cares about them, listens to them, and shares ideas with them. This relationship also gets them out of their homes for some exercise.
Family members are teachers and models.	
In group situations, young children learn what behaviors strengthen friendship and what behaviors cause problems.	
The peer group satisfies basic needs.	
Family relationships often satisfy basic human needs.	
Developing relationships with a variety of people helps you learn to accept differences among people.	
Social experiences with others can influence your emotional development.	

Relationships Throughout Life

Activity D

Chapter 9

Name _____

Date _____ Period _____

Interview four people who are in different age groups. Ask them to identify two people with whom they have a special relationship and to explain how they benefit from each relationship. Record what you learn in the space below.

Person interviewed: _Young child_

Description of special person:	Description of special person:
Parent	_Sister_
Benefits of relationship:	Benefits of relationship:
Takes care of me	_Teaches me_
Gives me what I need	_I have fun with her_
Loves me	

1. Person interviewed: _____

Description of special person:	Description of special person:
Benefits of relationship:	Benefits of relationship:

(Continued)

2. Person interviewed: _____

Description of special person:	Description of special person:
_____	_____
_____	_____
Benefits of relationship:	Benefits of relationship:
_____	_____
_____	_____
_____	_____
_____	_____

3. Person interviewed: _____

Description of special person:	Description of special person:
_____	_____
_____	_____
Benefits of relationship:	Benefits of relationship:
_____	_____
_____	_____
_____	_____
_____	_____

4. Person interviewed: _____

Description of special person:	Description of special person:
_____	_____
_____	_____
Benefits of relationship:	Benefits of relationship:
_____	_____
_____	_____
_____	_____
_____	_____

Effective Communication

Communication Skills

Name _____

Date _____ Period _____

Open communication involves the responsibility of being honest about your feelings without being rude or disrespectful. Suggest what might be said in each of the following situations to openly communicate in a respectful manner.

1. You are 16 years old. This afternoon, your father reprimanded you for not washing the car as you had promised. At that time, several of your father's friends were there to pick him up for a game of golf. You are embarrassed your father reprimanded you in front of his friends. How might you express your feelings to him when he returns home?

   _____

   _____

   _____

   _____

2. You confided in your friend Mary about something very personal. Another friend has just told you that Mary shared your secret with several people. What might you say to Mary?

   _____

   _____

   _____

   _____

3. Your brother has just come home from a shopping trip with a new pair of pants and a new shirt. You do not like the color combination. What might you say to your brother when he asks your opinion about the purchases?

   _____

   _____

   _____

   _____

4. You are standing at a bus stop with a group of friends who are making fun of an elderly woman standing near you. How might you be open with them to show your disagreement with what they are doing?

   _____

   _____

   _____

   _____

Using "I" Messages

Name _____

Date _____ Period _____

"I" messages can be helpful in conflict resolution. Briefly describe what "I" messages are and why they are helpful.

_____

_____

_____

Following each of these "you" messages, write an "I" message that would be more helpful in resolving the conflict.

1. You are so lazy. You haven't even cleaned up your room yet. _____

_____

_____

_____

_____

2. You are so insensitive. How could you treat me like that? _____

_____

_____

_____

_____

3. You are so rude. How could you talk to your brother like that? _____

_____

_____

_____

_____

4. You are too careless with the car, so I'm not going to let you use it. _____

_____

_____

_____

_____

5. You are so lazy. You could have helped your sister when she asked. _____

_____

_____

_____

_____

Conflict Resolution

Name _____

Date _____ Period _____

Think of a situation that could cause interpersonal conflict. Then follow the outline below to present the steps of positive conflict resolution.

1. Define the problem: _____

_____

_____

_____

2. Diagnose the cause: _____

_____

_____

_____

3. Change the problem to a goal: _____

_____

_____

4. Think of alternatives for reaching the goal and evaluate each alternative.

   Alternative A: _____

_____

_____

   Alternative B: _____

_____

_____

   Alternative C: _____

_____

_____

5. Choose the best alternative: _____

_____

_____

6. Describe a plan of action to reach the goal and solve the problem: _____

_____

_____

Your Communication Skills

Name _____

Date _____ Period _____

List six communication skills in the spaces indicated below. Think about each skill listed in terms of your own ability related to that skill. Then describe what steps you might take to improve that skill.

Communication Skill 1: _____

Steps to Improve: _____

_____

_____

_____

Communication Skill 2: _____

Steps to Improve: _____

_____

_____

_____

Communication Skill 3: _____

Steps to Improve: _____

_____

_____

_____

Communication Skill 4: _____

Steps to Improve: _____

_____

_____

_____

Communication Skill 5: _____

Steps to Improve: _____

_____

_____

_____

Communication Skill 6: _____

Steps to Improve: _____

_____

_____

_____

The Family Today

Families—Meeting Human Needs

Activity A	**Name** _____
Chapter 11	**Date** _____ **Period** _____

Below are listed five basic needs that are met by caring families. For each need listed, write one situation that illustrates how the family can meet the need for a child of any age and one situation that describes how the family can meet the need for a parent of any age.

Basic Needs	Meeting Basic Needs for a Child	Meeting Basic Needs for a Parent
1. Need for love		Example: When John Smith's elderly mother died, he was left with an empty feeling. The love provided by his wife and children helped comfort him.
2. Need for acceptance		
3. Need for feelings of self-worth		
4. Need for respect		
5. Need for recognition from others		

Change and Families

Name _____

Date _____ **Period** _____

List five changes, either societal or technological, that have occurred. In the space below, describe how this particular change has affected your family either positively or negatively.

1. Change:_____

   Effect: _____

   _____

   _____

   _____

   _____

2. Change:_____

   Effect: _____

   _____

   _____

   _____

   _____

3. Change:_____

   Effect: _____

   _____

   _____

   _____

   _____

4. Change:_____

   Effect: _____

   _____

   _____

   _____

   _____

5. Change:_____

   Effect: _____

   _____

   _____

   _____

   _____

A Family Who Cares

Name _____

Date _____ Period _____

Fill in the chart below with ways both a teenager and a parent could promote each characteristic of a caring family.

Characteristics of a Caring Family	How a Teenager Could Promote This Characteristic	How a Parent Could Promote This Characteristic
Family members are interdependent.		
Family members are responsible and trustful.		
Family members show respect and concern.		
Family members openly express and accept feelings.		
Family members are open to change.		

Family Crises

Name _____

Date _____ Period _____

Find an article in a newspaper or periodical related to family crises such as family violence, child abuse, substance abuse, divorce, or suicide. In the space below, include interesting information from the article to share with others in the class.

Title: _____

Author: _____

Source: _____

_____

_____

_____

_____

_____

_____

_____

_____

_____

_____

_____

_____

_____

_____

_____

_____

_____

_____

_____

_____

_____

_____

_____

_____

_____

_____

_____

The Marriage Relationship

Success Through the Years

Activity A

Chapter 12

Name _____

Date _____ Period _____

Interview four couples who have had successful marriages for at least 20 years. (You will also be interviewing these couples for Activity B.) Ask them to tell you why they feel their marriages have been a success. Record what you learn in the space below.

Couple 1

Couple 2

Couple 3

Couple 4

Analyze the responses given by the four couples. Were any of the reasons for success given by more than one couple? If so, what were these reasons?

_____

_____

_____

Marriage Adjustments

Name _____

Date _____ Period _____

Ask the same couples you interviewed in Activity A to tell you about some adjustments they made during the periods of time listed below.

1. The birth of their first child:

2. Their children's teen years:

3. When their children left home:

4. Their retirement years:

What other major and minor adjustments have they made through the years?

_____

_____

_____

_____

_____

Maturity and Marriage

Name _____

Date _____ Period _____

The overall maturity of a husband and wife strongly influences their chances for a successful marriage. Complete the chart below by describing a mature person and an immature person as related to each type of maturity.

Type of Maturity	Description of a Mature Person	Description of an Immature Person
Maturity as related to knowing and under-standing yourself		
Social maturity		
Emotional maturity		
Intellectual maturity		

What other major and minor adjustments have they made through the years?

_____

_____

_____

_____

_____

_____

Mutual Expectations About Marriage

Activity D

Chapter 12

Name _____

Date _____ Period _____

Serious conflicts can occur if a man and woman fail to share their expectations regarding marriage before they are married. This is especially true during this time of great social change and widely varying attitudes toward marriage. In the chart below, list two contrasting attitudes for each type of expectation.

Areas of Expectations	Attitude of First Person	Attitude of Second Person
Expectations regarding marriage as a commitment		
Expectations related to roles		
Expectations related to future goals		

Parenting

Assuming Parental Responsibilities

Name _____

Date _____ Period _____

Parents can assume their parental responsibilities in a variety of ways. Examples of two specific ways parents of teenagers might help them meet their physical needs are listed below.

   A. When Carl started a new job that involved working outside in the cold, his parents helped him buy a new pair of boots and heavy coat.

   B. Susan lives in a two-bedroom apartment with her parents and sister.

In the spaces provided, list two specific ways parents of teenagers might help teens meet their psychological needs.

1. Accepting and respecting the teenager
   A. _____
   _____
   _____
   B. _____
   _____
   _____

2. Caring for and loving the teenager
   A. _____
   _____
   _____
   B. _____
   _____
   _____

3. Helping the teenager build self-esteem
   A. _____
   _____
   _____
   B. _____
   _____
   _____

(Continued)

4. Providing opportunities to assume responsibilities

    A. _____

    _____

    _____

    B. _____

    _____

    _____

5. Transmitting values

    A. _____

    _____

    _____

    B. _____

    _____

    _____

6. Providing opportunity for growth

    A. _____

    _____

    _____

    B. _____

    _____

    _____

7. Guiding and disciplining

    A. _____

    _____

    _____

    B. _____

    _____

    _____

8. Encouraging independence

    A. _____

    _____

    _____

    B. _____

    _____

    _____

Parent-Child Communication

Name _____

Date _____ Period _____

Give an example of how a teenager could communicate each of the following to his or her parents.

1. A feeling of respect: _____

_____

_____

_____

2. A feeling of trust: _____

_____

_____

_____

3. A sense of responsibility: _____

_____

_____

_____

4. A feeling of openness: _____

_____

_____

_____

Give an example of how a parent might communicate each of the following to his or her child.

1. A feeling of respect: _____

_____

_____

_____

2. A feeling of trust: _____

_____

_____

_____

3. A sense of responsibility: _____

_____

_____

_____

4. A feeling of openness: _____

_____

_____

_____

Conflicting Views

Activity C

Chapter 13

Name _____

Date _____ **Period** _____

List four issues on which teens and parents often seem to have differing views. Considering what you have read in Chapter 13 about parent-child relationships, suggest ways that each might work to eliminate these differences.

1. Issue:_____

   Teen's viewpoint: _____

   _____

   _____

   _____

   Parent's viewpoint: _____

   _____

   _____

   _____

   Suggestions:_____

   _____

   _____

   _____

   _____

2. Issue:_____

   Teen's viewpoint: _____

   _____

   _____

   _____

   Parent's viewpoint: _____

   _____

   _____

   _____

   Suggestions:_____

   _____

   _____

   _____

   _____

3. Issue: _____

Teen's viewpoint: _____

_____

_____

Parent's viewpoint: _____

_____

_____

Suggestions: _____

_____

_____

_____

_____

4. Issue: _____

Teen's viewpoint: _____

_____

_____

Parent's viewpoint: _____

_____

_____

Suggestions: _____

_____

_____

_____

_____

Changes in Dependency

Activity D

Chapter 13

Name _____

Date _____ **Period** _____

Analyze the dependent, independent, and interdependent relationships that most of your friends have with their families. Then answer the questions listed below.

1. In what ways are most of your friends dependent on their families? Be specific.

_____

_____

_____

_____

_____

_____

_____

_____

2. In what ways do most of your friends show independence? Be specific.

_____

_____

_____

_____

_____

_____

_____

_____

3. Give examples of interdependence found in families with which you are familiar.

_____

_____

_____

_____

_____

_____

_____

_____

Family Management

Factors Affecting Family Management

Activity A

Chapter 14

Name _____

Date _____ Period _____

Read each situation described below and explain what factors in that situation are likely to affect management of the home and family.

Sharon is a 39-year-old woman whose husband was recently killed in an automobile accident. She has a 14-year-old daughter and a 16-year-old son. Sharon has been doing volunteer work at a local hospital.	
Mike, the youngest child in his family, will graduate from college this year. He has secured a teaching job in another state. His parents are pleased they have been able to provide their four children with a college education. At times, it seemed difficult to meet their financial challenges. However, with everyone contributing something to the family income, they were able to reach their goal.	
Kevin was recently laid off from his job at an automobile production plant. Although Kevin did not want his wife to work while their two children were of preschool age, she has been looking into job possibilities.	
Troy's brother is hospitalized with a very serious illness. Troy's sister-in-law spends day and night at the hospital to avoid the expense of having a private nurse. During this time, Troy's nieces, ages 10 and 15, and nephew, age 17, are staying with Troy and his wife, Marie. Troy and Marie do not have children of their own.	

Assuming Management Responsibilities

Name _____

Date _____ Period _____

Consider how assuming the following family responsibilities as a teenager could benefit you as an adult in your role as a single person, wife, husband, and/or parent. Explain the benefits of assuming each responsibility in the space provided.

Responsibilities Assumed as a Teenager	Resulting Benefits to You as an Adult
Taking care of younger brother or sister	
Doing the grocery shopping	
Helping make decisions about needs, wants, and priorities when discussing family spending	
Helping with the cooking and cleaning	
Helping with work outside the home, such as gardening, mowing the lawn, and making repairs	
Helping with remodeling, such as painting or wallpapering	

Sharing Family Management

Activity C

Name _____

Chapter 14

Date _____ **Period** _____

In the space provided, answer the following questions about sharing family management responsibilities.

1. Describe some ways both children and adults can benefit from sharing family responsibilities.

_____

_____

_____

_____

_____

_____

_____

_____

_____

2. Why is it so important that family members be given realistic responsibilities?

_____

_____

_____

_____

_____

_____

_____

_____

_____

3. What should families keep in mind when dividing responsibilities and setting standards for a completed task?

_____

_____

_____

_____

_____

_____

_____

_____

_____

A Family Management Plan

Activity D   **Name** _____

Chapter 14   **Date** _____ **Period** _____

Propose a plan for sharing management responsibilities within your own family. If you prefer, you may develop the plan for another family you know or a fictitious family. Give information about family composition and ages of family members, management tasks to be done, and your suggested plan.

_____

_____

_____

_____

_____

_____

_____

_____

_____

_____

_____

_____

_____

_____

_____

_____

_____

_____

_____

_____

_____

_____

_____

_____

_____

_____

_____

_____

_____

_____

_____

_____

_____

_____

Combining Family and Workplace Roles

Work Patterns

Name _____

Date _____ Period _____

The following are typical work patterns chosen by men and women. List possible pros and cons for each pattern. Then select the pattern you would most likely choose and explain why.

1. Husband and wife both work following school and pursue full-time careers. They begin their family in their late twenties.

Pros	Cons

2. One spouse is employed. The other spouse does not work at all following schooling. The couple have their children immediately after they marry.

Pros	Cons

3. One spouse leaves work when their children are born and resumes work following maternity or paternity leave.

Pros	Cons

4. One spouse leaves work when the children are born and resumes work when the children are older.

Pros	Cons

5. Which pattern would you choose? Explain your answer. _____

_____

_____

Impact of Family and Work on Each Other

Activity B   Name _____

Chapter 15   Date _____ Period _____

A better understanding of how family and work influence each other can be helpful in managing both roles. Read the following family description. In the chart below, describe how each of the possible events might affect the family and their work.

Tomas and Yolana are both employed outside the home. Tomas works for a large manufacturing company from 8-5, Monday through Friday. He rides to work with a neighbor who works for the same company. Yolana is a secretary in a medical office and works from 8:30-4:30, Monday through Friday. She drives their two children; ages 2 and 4, to child care on her way to work and picks them up after work. They feel fortunate that they both have good jobs, health insurance through their work, and a good child care situation for their children.

Possible events	Possible effects	
	on the family	on their work
Yolana has the flu and misses four days of work.		
The woman who cares for their children decides to retire and will no longer care for their two children.		
Tomas receives a promotion, which includes a substantial raise in his salary.		
Their car needs major repairs, which requires it be in the repair shop for two days.		
One of their children is sick with the measles.		

Responses to Family Needs

Activity C   Name _____

Chapter 15   Date _____ Period _____

The following are ways in which employers, governments, and communities are responding to the needs of working parents. Briefly explain how each of these might be helpful to families.

1. Flextime: _____

_____

_____

_____

_____

_____

_____

2. Flexplace: _____

_____

_____

_____

_____

_____

_____

3. Job sharing: _____

_____

_____

_____

_____

_____

_____

4. On-site child care center: _____

_____

_____

_____

_____

_____

_____

(Continued)

5. Benefit packages: _____

_____

_____

_____

_____

_____

_____

6. Family and medical leave: _____

_____

_____

_____

_____

_____

_____

7. School-based child care programs: _____

_____

_____

_____

_____

_____

_____

Skills Helpful in Combining Family and Work

Activity D

Chapter 15

Name _____

Date _____ Period _____

Below are listed skills parents can use to help them manage more effectively. Read each situation described below and decide which skill would be most helpful. Then explain how that skill will be helpful.

Decision-making skills

Skill in understanding your values and goals

Skill in recognizing resources available

Skill in time and energy management

Relationship skills

Attitude skills

1. Jimmy, age 8, is happy his mother finally found a good job because now they will be able to buy some things they could not afford before. However, he finds now she is so very busy with all she has to do that he misses the times they used to spend together.

Skill that would be helpful: _____

Explain: _____

_____

_____

_____

_____

_____

_____

_____

2. The Weber family has just moved to a new city as a result of a job transfer for Mr. Weber. Mrs. Weber will be starting a part-time job in two weeks. Their major challenge now is arranging for child care for their infant daughter and three-year-old son.

Skill that would be helpful: _____

Explain: _____

_____

_____

_____

_____

_____

_____

_____

(Continued)

3. Maria feels so very frustrated. Now that she is working full-time, she just can't seem to get everything done. She doesn't have time to keep her house as clean as she did before she started the job. She doesn't seem to have time to spend with her three children. Rarely do she and her husband have time to spend together.

Skill that would be helpful: _____

Explain: _____

_____

_____

_____

_____

_____

_____

_____

_____

_____

_____

4. Now that both their parents are working full-time, the three teenage children of Mike and Sara realize they could be doing more to help their parents. However, they aren't sure of just how to get organized.

Skill that would be helpful: _____

Explain: _____

_____

_____

_____

_____

_____

_____

_____

_____

_____

_____

Physical and Mental Wellness

Improving Health Habits

Activity A

Chapter 16

Name _____

Date _____ **Period** _____

Mentally healthy people tend to have certain qualities:

- They feel comfortable about themselves.
- They are able to balance independence and dependence.
- They can control their emotions.
- They are able to love.
- They are realistic.
- They are able to accept and adapt to change.

Based on the list of qualities above, evaluate your own mental health. Describe below how you might improve your mental health.

_____

_____

_____

_____

_____

_____

_____

_____

What you eat, your physical activity, and how much you sleep can have a large effect on your physical health. Use the space provided to record these activities for three days.

Day One
Eating habits:
Physical activity: **Sleep:**

(Continued)

Day Two

Eating habits:

Physical activity:	**Sleep:**

Day Three

Eating habits:

Physical activity:	**Sleep:**

Analyze your health habits. Are you eating right and getting enough exercise and sleep? In which areas do you need improvement?

Eating habits: _____

_____

_____

_____

Physical activity: _____

_____

_____

_____

Sleep: _____

_____

_____

_____

Factors Leading to Good Health

Name _____

Date _____ Period _____

Read each of the following statements. Circle *T* if the statement is true. Circle *F* if the statement is false. If a statement is false, correct it in the space provided.

T   F   1. Your health is most influenced by the many decisions you make daily. _____

_____

_____

T   F   2. Certain amounts and kinds of food materials are necessary to sustain physical life.

_____

_____

T   F   3. Nutrients are divided into five groups: carbohydrates, fats, proteins, minerals, and water.

_____

_____

T   F   4. Foods that are processed often contain large amounts of sugar and salt. _____

_____

_____

T   F   5. Exercise benefits the muscular and circulatory systems but does not affect how the heart, liver, brain, and lungs function. _____

_____

_____

T   F   6. Cautions related to physical activity programs are important. _____

_____

_____

T   F   7. During sleep, the body is busy recuperating and repairing itself, so body temperature goes up, breathing quickens, and blood pressure and pulse rate rise. _____

_____

_____

T   F   8. The amount of sleep people need is influenced mainly by rate of growth. _____

_____

_____

(Continued)

T F 9. The period of sleep right before you wake up is the deepest and the most refreshing.

_____

_____

_____

T F 10. Mentally healthy people are able to think for themselves and take responsibility for their own feelings and actions. _____

_____

_____

_____

T F 11. Mentally healthy people do not get angry. _____

_____

_____

_____

T F 12. Use of defense mechanisms indicates poor mental health. _____

_____

_____

_____

T F 13. Displacement occurs when a person counteracts a weakness by emphasizing a desirable characteristic. _____

_____

_____

_____

T F 14. Identification helps a person gain a feeling of self-worth. _____

_____

_____

_____

T F 15. Regression shifts the blame for an undesirable act to someone else. _____

_____

_____

_____

Researching Health Issues

Name _____

Date _____ Period _____

To a large extent, your health is affected by the way you live your life. The following are lifestyle issues about which people must make decisions:

- weight
- intake of fat, saturated fat, and cholesterol
- intake of salt
- use of sugar
- intake of foods with high fiber content
- use of alcohol
- use of other drugs
- smoking
- sexual behavior

Research current magazines and newspapers for an article related to one of the above topics. Then write a brief summary of that article in the space provided.

_____

_____

_____

_____

_____

_____

_____

_____

_____

_____

_____

_____

_____

_____

_____

_____

_____

_____

_____

_____

_____

Healthful Eating

The Functions of Food

Activity A

Chapter 17

Name _____

Date _____ Period _____

Answer the following questions related to the functions of food in the body.

1. List the three functions of food.

   A. _____

   B. _____

   C. _____

2. Muscle and bone consist mainly of what? _____

3. Name the two minerals that work with protein to build bones and teeth. _____

   _____

4. In addition to water, what else is needed to build blood?_____

   _____

   _____

5. Name the three body processes that nutrients control and coordinate. _____

   A. _____

   B. _____

   C. _____

6. Describe what happens during the digestion process. _____

   _____

   _____

   _____

7. Explain what enzymes are and how they function. _____

   _____

   _____

   _____

(Continued)

8. Describe what happens to nutrients during the process of absorption. _____

_____

_____

_____

9. List three metabolic processes that take place after food compounds have been absorbed into the bloodstream.

   A. _____

   _____

   B. _____

   _____

   C. _____

   _____

10. What is the function of hemoglobin? _____

_____

_____

_____

11. What are your body's three sources of energy? _____

   A. _____

   B. _____

   C. _____

12. What units indicate the amount of energy your body has burned? _____

Watching Your Diet

Name _____

Date _____ Period _____

Keep track of everything you eat for three days. Place each food in the proper category in the chart below. Total the amounts of food you ate each day from each food group. Then answer the questions on the next page.

	Day 1	**Day 2**	**Day 3**
Grains			
Totals:			
Vegetables			
Totals:			
Fruits			
Totals:			
Milk			
Totals:			
Meat and beans			
Totals:			
Oils			
Totals:			

(Continued)

1. For what food groups did you tend to consume less than the recommended amounts?

   _____

   _____

   _____

2. What could you add to your diet to meet the recommended amounts for these food groups?

   _____

   _____

   _____

3. For what food groups did you tend to consume more than the recommended amounts?

   _____

   _____

4. What could you cut out of your daily diet so you would meet the recommended amounts for these food groups? _____

   _____

   _____

5. How might you improve your eating habits to be sure your body gets the nutrients it needs?

   _____

   _____

   _____

   _____

   _____

   _____

Eating Out

Name _____

Date _____ **Period** _____

List a variety of foods a person might select at a fast-food restaurant in each of the following situations. Explain why these are good choices for that particular person.

1. A dinner for a teenager who is overweight and wants a filling meal without too many calories.

Selection: _____

_____

_____

Reasons for choosing each specific food: _____

_____

_____

_____

_____

2. A lunch for a person trying to avoid foods high in saturated fat and cholesterol.

Selection: _____

_____

_____

Reasons for choosing each specific food: _____

_____

_____

_____

_____

3. A dinner for someone who is trying to include more fiber in his or her diet.

Selection: _____

_____

_____

Reasons for choosing each specific food: _____

_____

_____

_____

_____

Positive Influences on Eating Habits

Name _____

Date _____ Period _____

Family members who prepare meals have a great influence on the eating habits of other family members. Describe how the following would be a positive influence on family members.

1. Carefully selecting and preparing foods to meet nutritional needs. _____

   _____

   _____

   _____

   _____

2. Having a positive attitude toward meal planning and preparation. _____

   _____

   _____

   _____

   _____

3. Selecting and serving a variety of foods. _____

   _____

   _____

   _____

   _____

4. Serving foods with a variety in color. _____

   _____

   _____

   _____

   _____

5. Serving foods with a variety of flavor. _____

   _____

   _____

   _____

   _____

6. Serving foods with a variety in texture. _____

   _____

   _____

   _____

   _____

Coping with Stress

Stress in Your Life

List five situations that have caused you stress in the past week.

1. _____
_____
2. _____
_____
3. _____
_____
4. _____
_____
5. _____
_____

Describe any physical reactions to stress that you noticed in each of the situations listed.

1. _____
2. _____
3. _____
4. _____
5. _____

Identify possible causes of stress in each of the five situations.

1. _____
_____
2. _____
_____
3. _____
_____
4. _____
_____
5. _____
_____

Managing Stress

Name _____

Date _____ Period _____

Choose one of the stressful situations identified in Activity A and use the problem-solving process as a step in coping with the stress.

1. Define the stress situation and identify the cause of the stress. _____

_____

_____

_____

_____

_____

_____

_____

_____

2. Develop at least three possible solutions to the problem. After each solution, indicate the pros and cons of that solution.

   A. _____

   _____

   _____

   _____

   _____

   _____

   B. _____

   _____

   _____

   _____

   _____

   _____

   C. _____

   _____

   _____

   _____

   _____

   _____

(Continued)

3. Choose the best solution and describe below a plan for carrying it out. Begin implementing the plan as soon as possible. _____

_____

_____

_____

_____

_____

4. Describe how you will evaluate the process used to manage this stressful situation. _____

_____

_____

_____

_____

_____

Personal Skills for Coping with Stress

Activity C

Chapter 18

Name _____

Date _____ Period _____

Make a list of stressful situations that have involved you personally. Analyze each situation and decide which personal skills listed in the following chart would have helped you deal with that stress if those skills had been further developed. Then place a check in the appropriate columns.

	Personal Skills for Coping with Stress								
Stressful Situations	Skill in Self-Observation	Skill in Value Clarification	Communication Skills	Attitude Skills	Organizational Skills	Skill in Maintaining Good Physical and Mental Health	Skill in Anticipating Stress	Time Management Skills	Relaxation Skills
Example: Being late for class.									

Analyze your list of stressful situations and your skills for coping with that stress. Choose one skill that could be further developed. Explain how you might do this.

_____

_____

_____

_____

_____

_____

_____

_____

Understanding Coping Skills

Activity D   **Name** _____

Chapter 18   **Date** _____ **Period** _____

Having a variety of personal coping skills will help you deal with stress. Following is a list of personal coping skills you may have or can develop. In the space provided, explain what each of these skills means in your own words.

1. Skill in self-observation:

 A. Viewing stressful situations in a positive way: _____

 _____

 _____

 B. Having healthy feelings about yourself: _____

 _____

 _____

 C. Developing healthy emotions: _____

 _____

 _____

 D. Having an open attitude toward change: _____

 _____

 _____

2. Skill in anticipating stress:_____

 _____

 _____

3. Personal management skills:

 A. Being able to clarify your values and prioritize your goals: _____

 _____

 _____

 B. Having flexible standards: _____

 _____

 _____

 C. Organizational skills: _____

 _____

 _____

(Continued)

D. Time management skills: _____

_____

_____

4. Relationship skills:

   A. Communication skills: _____

_____

_____

   B. Conflict resolution skills: _____

_____

_____

5. Skill in personal health and relaxation: _____

_____

_____

Environmental Responsibility

Hazardous Conditions

Name _____

Date _____ Period _____

The following chart lists hazardous conditions that people could prevent or lessen if they would take certain actions. For each hazardous condition, list three steps a person could take to make the environment safer and healthier.

Hazardous Condition	Actions Leading to a Safer and Healthier Environment
Air pollution	1. _____ _____ 2. _____ _____ 3. _____ _____
Water pollution	1. _____ _____ 2. _____ _____ 3. _____ _____
Noise pollution	1. _____ _____ 2. _____ _____ 3. _____ _____

(Continued)

Hazardous Condition	Actions Leading to a Safer and Healthier Environment
Pollution by solid waste materials	1. _____ _____ 2. _____ _____ 3. _____ _____
Pollution by radiation	1. _____ _____ 2. _____ _____ 3. _____ _____
Contamination of food	1. _____ _____ 2. _____ _____ 3. _____ _____
Motor vehicle accidents	1. _____ _____ 2. _____ _____ 3. _____ _____
Fire injuries and deaths	1. _____ _____ 2. _____ _____ 3. _____ _____

Resources for a Safer Environment

Activity B   **Name** _____

Chapter 19   **Date** _____ **Period** _____

Go through recent newspapers and find an article relating to an environmental concern. Then write a brief summary of the article.

Name of article: _____

Source of article: _____

_____

_____

_____

_____

_____

_____

_____

_____

_____

_____

_____

_____

_____

_____

_____

_____

_____

How might people use the above information as a resource to help make the environment safer?

_____

_____

_____

_____

_____

_____

_____

Staying Healthy

Activity C   **Name** _____

Chapter 19   **Date** _____ **Period** _____

Respond to the following questions.

1. What information is included in a health history? _____

_____

_____

2. For what reason has the annual physical exam become somewhat controversial? _____

_____

_____

_____

3. What tests should be performed once a year even if they are not part of a complete physical exam?

_____

_____

_____

4. What is the purpose of dental prophylaxis? _____

_____

_____

5. How do dentists find small cavities, decay beneath fillings, impacted teeth, and abnormal tooth roots?

_____

_____

_____

6. When should people with normal vision have their eyes examined? _____

_____

_____

7. How do vaccinations work to prevent diseases? _____

_____

_____

8. List warning signs of cancer. _____

_____

_____

9. List three signs of poor mental health. _____

_____

_____

10. What is the purpose of first aid? _____

_____

_____

Financial Management

Keeping Track of Your Records

Activity A

Chapter 20

Name _____

Date _____ Period _____

Describe a system of record keeping that would work well in your home. List the records you think your family should keep. Then describe the method you would use to organize them.

_____

_____

_____

_____

_____

_____

_____

_____

_____

_____

_____

_____

_____

_____

_____

_____

_____

_____

_____

_____

_____

_____

_____

_____

_____

_____

_____

_____

_____

_____

A Monthly Budget

Activity B　　　　　　　　　**Name** _____

Chapter 20　　　　　　　　　**Date** _____ **Period** _____

Tony and Maria are trying to revise their budget to include more savings for a new television set, which would cost about $500. They would like to develop a plan to save for five months for the new television. Their combined net monthly income is $2035. Tony and Maria are presently trying to put $100 in savings each month. This money is to be used for unforeseen expenses and also toward costs that will occur when they start a family.

Their present monthly budgeted amounts are as follows:

Rent . . . .$510　　Medical care . . . .$ 40
Food . . . . 320　　Leisure activities 180
Car insurance . . . . 85　　Clothing 120
Life insurance . . . . 25　　Personal care items 90
Car payments . . . . 330　　Gifts and contributions 60
Gas and oil . . . . 75　　Utilities 100
Savings 100

Their actual expenses for the past month are as follows:

Rent . . . .$510　　Medical care . . . .$ 52
Food . . . . 300　　Leisure activities 195
Car insurance . . . . 85　　Clothing 85
Life insurance . . . . 25　　Personal care items 80
Car payments . . . . 330　　Gifts and contributions 64
Gas and oil . . . . 88　　Utilities 100

Fill in the Monthly Budget on the next page. Then answer the following questions.

1. Complete the budget form using the figures given above. List fixed and flexible expenses in the appropriate columns and complete the columns labeled "Budgeted Amounts" and "Actual Amounts Spent."

What is the total of their budgeted amounts? _____

What is the total of the actual amount spent? _____

2. Next, determine whether Tony and Maria went over or under their budget in each category. Indicate this with either a " + " or " − " sign.

3. How would you revise this budget so that Tony and Maria would be able to include a budgeted amount toward buying a television? (They do not want to change their present $100 savings plan.) Indicate under "Revised Budget" your suggested changes and discuss below.

_____
_____
_____
_____
_____
_____
_____

(Continued)

Monthly Budget

Monthly net Income:	Budgeted amounts	Actual amounts spent	Amount over/under	Revised budget
Fixed expenses:				
_____				
_____				
_____				
_____				
_____				
_____				
_____				
_____				
_____				
Flexible expenses:				
_____				
_____				
_____				
_____				
_____				
_____				
_____				
Totals: (Sum of all fixed and flexible expenses.)				
Balance: (Subtract expenses from income.)				
Savings:				

Cash Spending

Name _____

Date _____ Period _____

Many people have no idea of where their money has gone over the past week or month. They do not have a record keeping system that allows them to account for the cash they spend. Decide on a system you could use to keep track of the cash you spend.

1. Describe the system you will use to account for your cash spending. _____

_____

_____

_____

_____

_____

_____

_____

_____

2. Try your system for a period of time, perhaps a week, two weeks, or a month. Then evaluate the system. How well did it work? Were you able to account for all your cash spending?

_____

_____

_____

_____

_____

_____

_____

_____

3. What changes, if any, should be made to improve the system? _____

_____

_____

_____

_____

_____

_____

_____

_____

Using Credit Wisely

Credit Advantages and Disadvantages

Activity A

Chapter 21

Name _____

Date _____ Period _____

Depending on how it is used, credit can be either an advantage or a disadvantage. Read the advantages and disadvantages listed below and develop a situation to illustrate how credit use can carry with it that advantage or disadvantage.

Advantages	Illustrations
Credit provides a temporary expansion of income to meet emergency needs.	
Credit allows people to purchase costly items that could not be purchased without using credit.	
Credit helps people when their income lags behind their expenses.	
Credit makes shopping more convenient.	

Disadvantages	Illustrations
Credit encourages overspending.	
Credit means additional expense.	
Credit encourages impulse buying.	

Types of Credit

Activity B   **Name** _____

Chapter 21   **Date** _____ **Period** _____

Answer the following questions related to various types of credit.

1. What is the difference between cash credit and sales credit? _____

   _____

   _____

2. Give a reason why a person might need cash credit. _____

   _____

   _____

3. Explain how a person who has an installment loan would repay the money owed. _____

   _____

   _____

4. Where might a person get sales credit? _____

   _____

   _____

5. When purchasing a product with installment credit, a contract is drawn up at the time of purchase. What information is included in this contract? _____

   _____

   _____

6. What is the purpose of making a cash down payment when buying on the installment plan?

   _____

   _____

7. What type of charge account is often used for everyday expenses, such as utilities, and carries with it no interest charge if the bill is fully paid in 30 days? _____

   _____

8. With what type of charge account do customers have a limited line of credit and the option of making additional purchases while money is still owed? _____

   _____

9. What may a seller do if you fail to pay for a product purchased with a credit card? _____

   _____

   _____

10. If you lose a credit card, what can you do to avoid being responsible for any unauthorized charges?

   _____

   _____

   _____

   _____

   _____

   _____

Obtaining Credit

Name _____

Date _____ Period _____

Assume that you are the credit manager of a department store. One of your duties is to investigate customers who want to open credit accounts with you. To make your decisions, you will need certain information about credit applicants. Some of the factors you will investigate are listed below. Each factor relates to one of the three C's of credit. Indicate whether each of the factors relates to character, capacity, or capital. Then explain how that factor might affect an applicant's credit rating.

1. Size of family is related to _____

   How might this factor affect an applicant's credit rating? _____

   _____

   _____

   _____

   _____

   _____

   _____

2. Property owned is related to _____

   How might this factor affect an applicant's credit rating? _____

   _____

   _____

   _____

   _____

   _____

   _____

3. Information about checking and savings accounts is related to _____

   How might this factor affect an applicant's credit rating? _____

   _____

   _____

   _____

   _____

   _____

   _____

(Continued)

4. Type of job and length of employment is related to _____

   How might this factor affect an applicant's credit rating? _____

   _____

   _____

   _____

   _____

   _____

5. Salary is related to _____

   How might this factor affect an applicant's credit rating? _____

   _____

   _____

   _____

   _____

   _____

6. Length of residence in the community is related to _____

   How might this factor affect an applicant's credit rating? _____

   _____

   _____

   _____

   _____

   _____

7. Number of loans and charge accounts and record of repayment is related to_____

   How might this factor affect an applicant's credit rating? _____

   _____

   _____

   _____

   _____

   _____

Consumer Credit Laws

Name _____

Date _____ Period _____

Fill in the charts on consumer credit laws by explaining the features of the laws and the benefits of the laws to consumers.

Truth in Lending Law	
Features of the Law	**Benefits to Consumers**

Equal Credit Opportunity Act	
Features of the Law	**Benefits to Consumers**

(Continued)

Fair Credit Reporting Act

Features of the Law	Benefits to Consumers

Fair Credit Billing Act

Features of the Law	Benefits to Consumers

Planning for Financial Security

Savings and Investment Choices

Activity A   **Name** _____

Chapter 22   **Date** _____ **Period** _____

Answer the following questions related to investments.

1. Describe the pros and cons of the following types of saving accounts:

   A. Passbook accounts. _____

   _____

   _____

   _____

   B. Time accounts. _____

   _____

   _____

   _____

   C. Money market accounts. _____

   _____

   _____

   _____

2. What will the Federal Deposit Insurance Corporation (FDIC) do if money in an insured bank account is lost or stolen? _____

   _____

3. What is liquidity? _____

   _____

   _____

4. What are the advantages in buying government savings bonds? _____

   _____

   _____

   _____

   _____

(Continued)

5. What knowledge can help you make investment decisions? _____

_____

_____

_____

6. Explain the differences between the following pairs of terms:

A. Savings and investing. _____

_____

_____

_____

_____

_____

B. Equity investments and fixed income investments. _____

_____

_____

_____

_____

_____

C. Preferred stock and common stock. _____

_____

_____

_____

_____

_____

7. Who issues municipal bonds, and why are they issued? _____

_____

_____

_____

8. What are dividends, and how might they be paid? _____

_____

_____

_____

9. What are mutual funds? _____

_____

_____

_____

Life Insurance Match

Name _____

Date _____ Period _____

Match the following terms to their appropriate descriptions.

_____ 1. General name for a type of life insurance that stays in force throughout the insured person's lifetime.

_____ 2. Type of permanent life insurance where the premiums are fixed but the face amount varies with the performance of invested funds.

_____ 3. The least costly type of permanent life insurance in which the amount of the premium is set when the policy is bought.

_____ 4. The sum of the savings that has built up in a permanent life insurance policy.

_____ 5. The person who receives the death benefit if the insured dies while the policy is in force.

_____ 6. Type of term life insurance where the premiums stay the same and the amount of coverage becomes smaller.

_____ 7. Type of permanent life insurance where the policy-holder makes payments for a certain number of years and then receives the face value of the policy.

_____ 8. Type of life insurance that stays in force only for a specific period of time.

_____ 9. Type of term insurance that a policyholder can exchange for permanent life insurance within a given period of time without having a medical exam.

_____ 10. Life insurance that covers the repayment of a loan if the borrower dies.

_____ 11. Term life insurance that maintains a certain amount of protection throughout the term and maintains a fixed death benefit.

_____ 12. The premiums, face value, and level of protection of this form of permanent life insurance can be altered as needed; the cash value is invested.

_____ 13. A type of permanent life insurance in which the policy-holder pays premiums for only a certain length of time and the face value is paid only in the event of death.

_____ 14. Type of term life insurance that allows the policyholder to extend the policy beyond the first term without having a medical examination.

_____ 15. An extremely flexible type of permanent life insurance that can be altered in many ways by the policyholder.

A. convertible term life insurance

B. decreasing term life insurance

C. level term life insurance

D. credit life insurance

E. term life insurance

F. variable life insurance

G. beneficiary

H. universal life insurance

I. cash value

J. adjustable life insurance

K. whole life insurance

L. limited payment life insurance

M. endowment life insurance

N. permanent life insurance

O. renewable term life insurance

Automobile Insurance

Activity C

Chapter 22

Name _____

Date _____ **Period** _____

Conduct some research to find out about financial responsibility laws in your state. Then summarize what you have learned. _____

_____

_____

_____

_____

The itemized cost of insurance for a family's two autos for a period of six months is listed below. Study the figures and answer the questions that follow.

2003 Compact car

100/300 Bodily Injury Liability	138.20
Property Damage Liability	56.10
100/300 Uninsured Motorist Bodily Injury	56.20
2,000 Medical Expense	12.00
Nondeductible Comprehensive Physical Damage	28.00
100 Deductible Collision	75.20
Total Premium	$ 365.70

2006 Full-size car

100/300 Bodily Injury Liability	151.20
Property Damage Liability	61.10
100/300 Uninsured Motorist Bodily Injury	56.20
2,000 Medical Expense	12.00
Nondeductible Comprehensive Physical Damage	44.00
100 Deductible Collision	107.00
Total Premium	$ 431.50

1. Which form of coverage is the most expensive? Give figures to support your answer. _____

   _____

   _____

2. Why might the family decide not to have collision coverage on the 2003 car? _____

   _____

   _____

3. Based on the figures you see on these two vehicles, what would be the total amount of premiums for one year? _____

4. Why would this family choose to have $100 deductible collision coverage on the 2003 car rather than having full collision coverage? _____

   _____

   _____

   _____

Understanding Insurance

Name _____

Date _____ Period _____

In the space provided, explain how the following terms differ.

1. Term insurance vs. permanent insurance:

_____

_____

_____

_____

2. Group insurance vs. individual insurance:

_____

_____

_____

_____

3. Basic medical coverage vs. major medical coverage:

_____

_____

_____

_____

4. HMOs vs. PPOs:

_____

_____

_____

_____

5. Medicare vs. Medicaid:

_____

_____

_____

_____

6. Replacement cost vs. actual cash value:

_____

_____

_____

_____

Retirement Plans

Name _____

Date _____ Period _____

Interview people of three different ages about their retirement plans. Interview one person who has already retired, one person who will be retiring soon, and one person in his or her twenties. To prepare for the interview, form small groups and develop a separate set of questions for each person you will interview. Plan to ask each person four questions that are appropriate for a person in that age group. Write the questions you will ask in the space below and then fill in the answers you receive during the interviews.

Interview with Retired Person

Question #1 _____:

_____

_____

Answer:_____

_____

_____

Question #2: _____

_____

_____

Answer:_____

_____

_____

Question #3: _____

_____

_____

Answer:_____

_____

_____

Question #4: _____

_____

_____

Answer:_____

_____

_____

(Continued)

Interview with Person Who Will Retire Soon

Question #1 _____

_____

_____

Answer:_____

_____

_____

Question #2: _____

_____

_____

Answer:_____

_____

_____

Question #3: _____

_____

_____

Answer:_____

_____

_____

Question #4: _____

_____

_____

Answer:_____

_____

_____

(Continued)

Interview with Person in His or Her Twenties

Question #1 _____

_____

_____

Answer:_____

_____

_____

Question #2: _____

_____

_____

Answer:_____

_____

_____

Question #3: _____

_____

_____

Answer:_____

_____

_____

Question #4: _____

_____

_____

Answer:_____

_____

Consumer Rights and Responsibilites

Your Rights Protected

Activity A   Name _____

Chapter 23   Date _____ Period _____

Choose one of the following groups that protect consumer rights and research it thoroughly. Then write a brief report on what that group does to protect consumers.

Better Business Bureaus   Federal Trade Commission
Consumer Product Safety Commission   Food and Drug Administration
Department of Agriculture   Office of Consumer Affairs
Environmental Protection Agency   Public Health Service

_____

_____

_____

_____

_____

_____

_____

_____

_____

_____

_____

_____

_____

_____

_____

_____

_____

_____

_____

_____

_____

_____

_____

Persuasive Advertising

Name _____

Date _____ Period _____

Look through recent magazines and find four examples of persuasive advertisements. List the product or service advertised and the technique of persuasive advertising used. Describe what, if any, helpful information is included in the advertisement. Bring the advertisements to class and discuss them with other class members.

Product or Service Advertised	Technique Used	Helpful Information Included
1.		
2.		
3.		
4.		

The Responsible Consumer

Activity C

Chapter 23

Name _____

Date _____ **Period** _____

If consumers expect to receive quality products, they have the responsibility to read and follow the manufacturer's recommendations included with a product.

Read the use and care booklets put out by the manufacturers of three different appliances. (If you do not have these booklets in your home, you may be able to obtain them from a store that sells appliances.) In the space below, describe information in the booklet that is important to the proper functioning of the appliance. Also indicate any information with which you were totally unfamiliar that would help you to use and care for the appliance properly.

Appliance #1:

Appliance #2:

Appliance #3:

Consumer Complaints

Activity D

Chapter 23

Name _____

Date _____ Period _____

Think of a consumer problem you or someone you know has had recently. If you do not know of an actual incident, you may make up a consumer problem that could occur. In the space provided, write a complaint letter to the appropriate person. Be sure to include all details of the problem as discussed in the text.

_____

_____

_____

_____

_____

_____

_____

_____

_____

_____

_____

_____

_____

_____

_____

_____

_____

_____

_____

_____

_____

_____

_____

_____

_____

_____

_____

_____

_____

Consumer Decision Making

Economic Research

Activity A   **Name** _____

Chapter 24   **Date** _____ **Period** _____

Look through current newspapers or magazines or surf the Internet to find an article that relates to the topic of economics. The article may discuss any related topic, such as the United States economy or economic growth. Read the article and complete the following report. Discuss your article with others in class.

1. Title of article: _____

2. Source of article: _____

3. Main topic of article: _____

    _____

4. Write a brief statement summarizing the main points of the article.

    _____

    _____

    _____

    _____

    _____

    _____

    _____

    _____

    _____

5. Explain how this article related to the average consumer.

    _____

    _____

    _____

    _____

    _____

    _____

    _____

    _____

Our Economic System

Activity B

Chapter 24

Name _____

Date _____ Period _____

Characteristics of our economic system are listed below. Give an example from daily living to illustrate each characteristic in action. Then explain the advantages of each characteristic to people living in the United States.

Right to Private Property	
Example:	**Advantages:**

Profit Motivation	
Example:	**Advantages:**

Competition	
Example:	**Advantages:**

Freedom of Choice	
Example:	**Advantages:**

Consumer Decision Making in Action

Activity C   **Name** _____

Chapter 24   **Date** _____ **Period** _____

Show your understanding of the consumer decision-making process by using this process to make a consumer decision.

1. Define the problem: _____

_____

_____

2. Choose three possible alternatives:

    A. _____

       _____

    B. _____

       _____

    C. _____

       _____

3. Weigh the costs and benefits of each alternative to find the best choice:

    A. _____

       _____

    B. _____

       _____

    C. _____

       _____

4. Which alternative will you choose? _____

5. Evaluate the choice and review the process:

_____

_____

_____

_____

_____

_____

_____

_____

_____

_____

_____

Evaluating the Decision

Activity D   **Name** _____

Chapter 24   **Date** _____ **Period** _____

Evaluating the consumer decision-making process is a way to gain information that will help improve your skill in making decisions. Through evaluation, you can learn which step in the process may have led to a poor decision. You can then work on gaining skill in that step of the process.

Think of an instance in which you know a poor consumer decision was made and describe it below. The situation may be from personal experience or from the experience of family members and other people you know. Analyze the decision-making process used and answer the questions below. If you are using another person's experience, you will need to learn the process that led that person to make his or her decision.

Evaluation of Decision

1. Describe the consumer decision: _____

   _____

   _____

   _____

   _____

2. Which step in the decision-making process led to this decision? _____

   _____

   _____

   _____

   _____

3. How could this step have been handled differently to produce better results? _____

   _____

   _____

   _____

   _____

4. How could the knowledge gained from this situation be used to make better consumer decisions in the future? _____

   _____

   _____

   _____

Meal Management—Planning and Shopping

Advertised Specials

Name _____

Date _____ Period _____

Look through a local newspaper and find an advertisement for a large supermarket. Using the advertised specials as a basis, plan two meals of your choice. Write out the menus for both meals and make shopping lists of items you would need to buy to prepare the meals. Attach the advertisement to this page and circle the specials you plan to buy.

Menu for First Meal

Shopping List for First Meal

(Continued)

Menu for Second Meal

Shopping List for Second Meal

Efficient Meal Planning

Name _____

Date _____ Period _____

Tom and Cathy Green both get home from work at about 5:15 in the evening. On Thursday, they both have a meeting at 7:30. They would like to eat dinner by 6:15 so they will have time to get ready for their meetings. Using the moderate meal pattern for dinner listed below to guide you, plan a meal that can be prepared in 45 minutes. Use at least one timesaving piece of equipment, at least one convenience food, and some advance preparation. Describe the meal you plan in the space provided, and then answer the questions about the meal plan.

Moderate Meal Plan for Dinner

Meat, poultry, or fish   Salad

Potato, rice, or pasta   Bread

Vegetable   Beverage

Menu for Dinner	Description of Preparation Required

What time-saving piece of equipment will be used? Explain. _____

_____

_____

_____

What convenience food? _____

_____

_____

_____

Describe the advance preparation that will be done. _____

_____

_____

_____

Efficient Grocery Shopping

Activity C

Chapter 25

Name _____

Date _____ Period _____

Grocery shopping can be done more efficiently if the list is made in the order that foods appear in the store. Visit the grocery store where your family usually shops and draw a diagram of the store in the space provided. Label the sections where the various types of foods are found, such as baking supplies, meats, produce, breads, canned foods, and frozen foods.

Unit Pricing

Activity D

Chapter 25

Name _____

Date _____ Period _____

Unit pricing allows you to easily compare the prices of products available in different sizes of packages and cans. Go to a food store that uses unit pricing and select two products that are available in a national name brand, a house or store brand, and a generic brand. The products should all be in the same form, such as canned or frozen, and similar in size. Describe the products you have chosen and how you intend to use them. Then use unit pricing to compare the cost of the three different brands. Fill in the charts below with the brand name of the products and the information listed on the unit pricing tag. Then decide which brand would be the best buy.

Product description and intended use: _____

_____

	Brand of Product	**Information on Unit Pricing Tag**
National Name Brand		
Store or House Brand		
Generic Brand		

Based on the unit pricing information and your intended use of the product, which brand would be the best buy and why? _____

_____

_____

_____

_____

_____

_____

(Continued)

Name _____

Product description and intended use: _____

_____

	Brand of Product	Information on Unit Pricing Tag
National Name Brand		
Store or House Brand		
Generic Brand		

Based on the unit pricing information and your intended use of the product, which brand would be the best buy and why? _____

_____

_____

_____

_____

_____

_____

Deciding Where to Shop

Name _____

Date _____ Period _____

Food is sold in a variety of stores. List the advantages and disadvantages of shopping in each type listed in the chart below.

Type of Store	Advantages	Disadvantages
Supermarket		
Smaller, independent neighborhood stores		
Warehouse stores		
Specialty stores		
Food cooperatives		

Choose three food items you could purchase at each of the stores listed above. Try to visit three of these store types and compare the prices of the exact same items in each location.

Name of Store	Product #1: _____	Product #2: _____	Product #3: _____
	Price:	Price:	Price:
	Price:	Price:	Price:
	Price:	Price:	Price:

In which type of store would you prefer to shop? _____ Why? _____

_____

_____

_____

Using Leftovers to Avoid Waste

Name _____

Date _____ Period _____

Assume that there are leftovers from each of the main dishes in the far left column. Complete the chart with one way you could use each leftover in a dinner and one way you could use each leftover in a lunch.

Main Dish	Leftovers Used in a Dinner	Leftovers Used in a Lunch
Beef roast		
Roasted chicken		
Baked fish		
Baked ham		

Meal Preperation

Storage in the Kitchen

Activity A

Chapter 26

Name _____

Date _____ Period _____

In the space below, draw a diagram showing the preparation, cooking and serving, and cleanup centers of a kitchen.

Read through the list of kitchen equipment below and decide whether each item should be stored in the preparation center, the cooking and serving center, or the cleanup center. Then write the letter of the correct answer in the blank. Some equipment could be stored in more than one work center.

A. preparation center
B. cooking and serving center
C. cleanup center

_____ 1. Dinner plates.

_____ 2. Dish towels.

_____ 3. Rubber spatula.

_____ 4. Pot holders.

_____ 5. Grater.

_____ 6. Colander.

_____ 7. Electric mixer.

_____ 8. Paring knife.

_____ 9. Refrigerator storage containers.

_____ 10. Cutting board.

_____ 11. Pots and pans.

_____ 12. Electric frypan.

_____ 13. Measuring spoons.

_____ 14. Napkins.

_____ 15. Mixing bowls.

_____ 16. Stainless steel flatware.

_____ 17. Dishwashing detergent.

_____ 18. Aluminum foil and wax paper.

_____ 19. Vegetable peeler.

_____ 20. Cookie sheet.

A Time Plan for Meal Preparation

Name _____

Date _____ Period _____

Mike now lives in his own apartment. He has invited his parents over for dinner to show them what a good cook he has become. Mike gets home from work at 4:45 in the afternoon and plans to eat at 6:15. Decide on a menu for the dinner. Then develop a time plan for Mike to follow in preparing the meal for himself and his parents. Write out the recipes to be used in the space below.

Menu

Steps in Preparation	Time Allowed for Preparation Steps

Recipes

Preparation Techniques

Name _____

Date _____ Period _____

Read each of the following situations and suggest cooking procedures that would eliminate possible problems.

1. Suzanne is making hot chocolate for some friends she has invited to her home after a football game. She is making it a quick and easy way by heating milk and chocolate syrup together. Suzanne hopes it will turn out smooth and creamy. Sometimes the hot chocolate she makes is lumpy and has a film on top. What suggestions do you have for Suzanne?

_____

_____

_____

_____

_____

_____

2. Bob is planning to fix his girlfriend, Heidi, her favorite cake, angel food, for her birthday. He is worried because the only other time he tried to make an angel food cake, it flopped. The egg whites just didn't beat well. What suggestions could you give Bob to help him get good volume from the egg whites?

_____

_____

_____

_____

_____

_____

3. Maria called her sister for some advice. Something is wrong with her range, so she must do all her cooking in the wall oven until the range is repaired. Maria has the use of her broiler along with regular oven heat. Maria needs some ideas of how she can fix meat in her oven for the next three nights. Give Maria three suggestions for how to use her oven to prepare the main dish. Briefly describe each of the methods.

_____

_____

_____

_____

_____

_____

Avoiding Problems in Preparation

Activity D

Chapter 26

Name _____

Date _____ Period _____

The chart below lists several common problems in food preparation. In the column on the right, explain how each problem could be prevented.

Problem	How To Avoid the Problem
1. Gravy is lumpy.	
2. Muffins are very tough.	
3. When frying meat, the margarine used turns brown and smokes.	
4. Fruit turns dark after being sliced.	
5. Fruits, such as apples, shrivel up when cooked.	
6. Green vegetables change to a dull color when cooked.	

Retaining Nutrients in Food

Activity E

Chapter 26

Name _____

Date _____ Period _____

Use your text and one other reliable source of nutrition information to develop a list of procedures that are helpful in retaining nutrients. List five procedures that were in the text and five procedures from the other source. Discuss your list with other class members.

1. _____

    _____

2. _____

    _____

3. _____

    _____

4. _____

    _____

5. _____

    _____

6. _____

    _____

7. _____

    _____

8. _____

    _____

9. _____

    _____

10. _____

    _____

Understanding Heat

Activity F   **Name** _____

Chapter 26   **Date** _____ **Period** _____

Complete the following sentences related to the significance of heat in cooking by writing the correct word or words in the blanks.

1. Cooking involves the transfer of heat to the _____ being heated.

2. Food may be heated through conduction, _____, convection, or microwaves.

3. When heat travels by _____, it moves from the heat source to the bottom of the pan, to the substance being heated.

4. With _____ heating, circulating currents of hot air heat the food product.

5. With convection cooking, heating is more uniform in the _____ of the oven.

6. Foods do not brown or become crisp when cooked in the _____.

7. The greatest advantage of microwave cooking is _____ _____
   _____.

8. _____ utensils are not normally used in the microwave.

9. _____, _____ and _____ are good conductors
   of heat.

10. _____ and _____ are poor conductors of heat.

11. Cookware that has a dark or rough, dull surface tends to be more efficient than brightly polished cookware because it is a good _____ of radiant energy.

12. Cookware with a _____ surface tends to cook foods less efficiently.

13. The _____ of the metal affects the efficiency of cookware.

14. Foods absorb heat at different rates largely due to their _____
    _____.

Planning and Shopping for Clothes

The Significance of Clothing

Activity A

Chapter 27

Name _____

Date _____ **Period** _____

Describe a specific situation in which clothing selection could be influenced by each of the following factors.

1. Need for protection: _____

_____

_____

_____

2. Need for comfort: _____

_____

_____

_____

3. Desire to make a good first impression: _____

_____

_____

_____

4. Desire for social approval: _____

_____

_____

_____

5. Desire to be different: _____

_____

_____

_____

_____

(Continued)

6. Desire to have status: _____

_____

_____

_____

_____

7. Your personality: _____

_____

_____

_____

_____

8. Your values: _____

_____

_____

_____

_____

A Clothing Inventory

Name _____

Date _____ Period _____

Complete a clothing inventory. Attach an additional sheet of paper if needed. Summarize your findings by answering the question below. Use this inventory to develop a list of clothing needs.

Clothes/Accessories	Description (Colors/Fabrics)	Keep	Repair/Alter	Discard

What have you learned about the status of your current wardrobe? _____

_____

_____

_____

Clothing needs: _____

_____

_____

_____

Elements of Design

Name _____

Date _____ **Period** _____

Answer the questions below and select an outfit that uses line, color, and texture in a way that would be attractive on you.

1. Describe one of your clothing needs. For instance, you might need a new casual outfit, such as new jeans and a sweater for school. Perhaps you might need a more formal outfit for an upcoming dance. _____

   _____

   _____

   _____

2. In one sentence, describe your body type. _____

   _____

   _____

3. Based on your body type, describe how you could use line, color, and texture in clothing to help you look your best. _____

   _____

   _____

   _____

   _____

   _____

   _____

4. Look through catalogs and magazines to find a picture of an outfit that would meet your clothing need and would look attractive on you. Keep in mind the descriptions of line, color, and texture that you have listed. Mount the picture in the space below.

Knowledge and Skill in Clothing Selection

Activity D

Chapter 27

Name _____

Date _____ Period _____

Describe a garment, such as a blouse, shirt, pants, skirt, or dress that you would like to purchase.

_____

_____

Select four fabric samples from the box of samples in the classroom and mount them in the space provided. Beneath each piece of fabric, explain why it would or would not be a good choice for the garment you listed.

_____   _____
_____   _____
_____   _____
_____   _____
_____   _____
_____   _____
_____   _____

(Continued)

28

Caring for Clothing

Your Clothing Care Habits

Name _____

Date _____ Period _____

Rate yourself according to how well you care for your clothing. Read each statement and place a check in the appropriate column.

Usually	Sometimes	Never	
_____	_____	_____	1. I hang up my clothes when I take them off.
_____	_____	_____	2. I fold knitted garments and store them properly.
_____	_____	_____	3. I store my clothes so that my closet and dresser are neat and orderly.
_____	_____	_____	4. I remove spots and stains before garments are washed.
_____	_____	_____	5. I follow the care label on garments for laundering or dry cleaning.
_____	_____	_____	6. I store only clean clothes. Stained clothing is washed or dry cleaned.

For three days, keep track of what you do to care for your clothing. Jot down notes each day on routine care of clothing, clothing storage, clothing repair, and the laundering of clothing. Record your notes in the space provided.

Day 1

(Continued)

Day 2

Day 3

Analyze the way you care for your clothing. Did you take all the steps in clothing care that you should have taken? What might you do to improve the way you care for clothing? _____

_____

_____

_____

_____

_____

_____

_____

Clothing Storage

Activity B

Chapter 28

Name _____

Date _____ Period _____

Cut out pictures from catalogs, magazines, or newspapers or draw sketches of various products available for storing clothing or accessories. Mount the pictures on this page.

Care Labels

Name _____

Date _____ Period _____

Check the care labels on several types of garments in your wardrobe. Then use the information you find on six of those labels to fill in the chart below.

Type of Garment	Fiber Content	Proper Care of Garment
1.		
2.		
3.		
4.		
5.		
6.		

Were there any instructions on the care labels that you did not understand? If so, list them here and discuss them with others in the class. _____

_____

_____

_____

_____

_____

A Comparison of Laundry Products

Name _____

Date _____ Period _____

Compare the information on four different laundry products used to keep your clothes clean. Use the information to complete this chart. Compare your chart with those of other class members.

	Product 1	Product 2	Product 3	Product 4
Product Name				
Name of manufacturer				
Cost per use of product				
Performance claims				
Directions for use				
Special precautions				
Other helpful information				

(Continued)

Based upon the information in the chart on the previous page, which laundry product would you like to try? Explain why.

_____
_____
_____
_____
_____
_____
_____
_____
_____
_____
_____
_____
_____
_____
_____
_____
_____
_____
_____
_____
_____
_____
_____
_____
_____
_____
_____
_____
_____
_____
_____
_____

Planning and Selecting Housing

Homes Meeting Human Needs

Name _____

Date _____ Period _____

The left column of the chart below lists human needs that are influenced by housing. In the right column, explain how housing and home furnishings can help satisfy each of those needs.

Human Needs	Ways the Home Can Help Satisfy Human Needs
Good health	
Comfort	
Personal safety	
Interaction with others	
Security	
Space needs	

Factors Affecting Housing Satisfaction

Activity B Name _____

Chapter 29 Date _____ Period _____

Interview a family other than your own about their satisfaction with their housing. Describe the family in the space below. Then answer the questions that follow.

Write a description of the family interviewed. Include how many family members there are. List their ages, abilities, hobbies, and interests. Include any other information about the family that you feel is important.

_____

_____

_____

_____

_____

_____

_____

_____

_____

1. How would you describe the building design and site of the family's home? Is the family satisfied with the building design and site? Why or why not? _____

_____

_____

_____

_____

_____

_____

2. How would you describe the orientation of the home? Is the family satisfied with the orientation of their home? _____

_____

_____

_____

_____

_____

_____

(Continued)

3. What facts about the community influence the family's satisfaction with their home? Is the community a positive or negative influence on their satisfaction? _____

_____

_____

_____

_____

_____

4. What protective restrictions, such as zoning laws and codes, exist in the family's community? Do they feel these restrictions are good or bad? Explain. _____

_____

_____

_____

_____

_____

5. What are the positive and negative aspects of the neighborhood in which the family lives? Is the family basically satisfied or dissatisfied with their neighborhood? _____

_____

_____

_____

_____

_____

6. Overall, do you feel this family is satisfied with their housing? Explain why or why not. _____

_____

_____

_____

_____

_____

Rental Considerations

Name _____

Date _____ Period _____

Discuss leases with three people who have rented housing. In the space provided, summarize their comments and suggestions related to each subject.

What to Consider Before Renting	Comments and Suggestions of Renters
Lease contents	
Lease period	
Renewal option	
Clauses within the lease	
Amount of security deposit	
Refund of security deposit	
Other comments or suggestions	

Housing Alternatives

Name _____

Date _____ Period _____

List what you believe are the advantages and disadvantages of each type of housing listed below.

Types of Housing	Advantages	Disadvantages
Single-family home		
Manufactured home		
Condominium		
Cooperative		
Apartment		

Financing a Home Purchase

Name _____

Date _____ Period _____

A variety of options for financing a home are listed below. List their advantages and disadvantages.

Financing Options	Advantages	Disadvantages
FHA-insured loan		
VA-guaranteed loan		
Conventional loan		
Land contract		

Furnishing and Caring for the Home

Design in Home Furnishings

Activity A

Chapter 30

Name _____

Date _____ **Period** _____

Look through magazines to find a picture of a room that you find attractive and mount it in the space below. Then analyze the use of design in the room.

Analyze the use of design in the room pictured above. Comment on the use of the elements of design, color schemes, and the principles of design. _____

_____

_____

_____

_____

_____

_____

_____

_____

_____

_____

Color Schemes

Name _____

Date _____ Period _____

Find pictures of rooms decorated using the following color schemes: monochromatic, accented neutral, analogous, and complementary. Mount the pictures in the space provided. Define each color scheme and list the colors that are used in each room.

Monochromatic color scheme: _____

_____

_____

_____

Accented neutral: _____

_____

_____

_____

(Continued)

[blank box]

Analogous color scheme: _____

_____

_____

_____

[blank box]

Complementary color scheme: _____

_____

_____

_____

Chapter 30 Furnishing and Caring for the Home **163**

Selecting Home Furnishings

Name _____

Date _____ Period _____

Gather information on selecting one type of home furnishing. You may use books, magazines, interviews, and visits to businesses to do your research. Write a brief report explaining what you feel is important to consider in making this type of selection. Choose from the furnishings listed below.

1. Carpet
2. Wood furniture
3. Upholstered furniture
4. Wall treatments

5. Windows
6. Window treatments
7. Lighting
8. Accessories

Selection of _____

Information needed to make a wise decision.

_____
_____
_____
_____
_____
_____
_____
_____
_____
_____
_____
_____
_____
_____
_____
_____
_____
_____
_____
_____
_____
_____
_____
_____

(Continued)

Preventive Maintenance

Name _____

Date _____ Period _____

Many tasks done routinely in the home are actually steps in preventive maintenance. List six tasks that fall into this category and tell what damage might occur if these tasks are not done.

Tasks That Are Part of Preventive Maintenance	DamageThat Could Occur If Tasks Are Not Done
1.	
2.	
3.	
4.	
5.	
6.	

Career Planning

Attitudes Toward Careers

Activity A
Chapter 31

Name _____

Date _____ Period _____

Recall experiences in your life that have given you either a positive attitude or a negative attitude toward various types of careers. Then explain how these attitudes might influence your career planning. Share this information with others in the class. One example has been listed for you.

Experience and Attitude Developed	Effect on Career Planning
Example: My sixth grade math teacher was my favorite teacher during all of my grade school years. I really liked him and did very well in math that year.	This experience made me think I might like to become a math teacher.

Knowing Yourself

Name _____

Date _____ Period _____

Conduct your own self-study in relation to career plans by responding to each of the following.

1. INTERESTS: List the interests that are most important to you and classify them in some way.

   _____

   _____

   _____

   _____

   _____

2. ABILITIES: Describe your abilities that indicate skills and activities that you can perform successfully.

   _____

   _____

   _____

   _____

   _____

3. ACHIEVEMENTS: List your achievements and the skills you used in each accomplishment.

   _____

   _____

   _____

   _____

   _____

4. PERSONAL CHARACTERISTICS: Describe your personal traits and habits that would be important to consider in career planning. _____

   _____

   _____

   _____

   _____

   _____

5. SUMMARY: Review what you have written and list several careers that might be satisfying to you.

   _____

   _____

   _____

   _____

   _____

Specific Knowledge About Careers

Activity C

Chapter 31

Name _____

Date _____ **Period** _____

Select two career options that interest you and research them carefully. You may want to use interviews as well as library research to obtain your information. Fill in the information you learn about each career.

Career Option #1: _____

Employment outlook for the future: _____

_____

Approximate salary range: _____

Opportunities for advancement: _____

_____

_____

Training and/or education required: _____

_____

_____

Skills and knowledge required: _____

_____

_____

Duties and responsibilities: _____

_____

_____

_____

Positive and negative aspects of career: _____

_____

_____

_____

Other comments: _____

_____

_____

_____

Based on what you have learned about this career, does it still interest you? Why or why not? _____

_____

_____

_____

(Continued)

Career Option #2: _____

Employment outlook for the future: _____
_____

Approximate salary range: _____

Opportunities for advancement: _____
_____
_____

Training and/or education required: _____
_____
_____

Skills and knowledge required: _____
_____
_____

Duties and responsibilities: _____
_____
_____
_____
_____

Positive and negative aspects of career: _____
_____
_____
_____
_____

Other comments: _____
_____
_____
_____
_____

Based on what you have learned about this career, does it still interest you? Why or why not? _____
_____
_____
_____
_____

Jobs Involving Management

Activity D　　　　　　　　**Name** _____

Chapter 31　　　　　　　　**Date** _____ **Period** _____

Refer to the chart on management careers in your text and select two jobs that interest you from each level. Then write a brief paragraph explaining how management is a part of each job.

Jobs Requiring a High School Diploma

Job Title	How Job Involves Management
A.	
B.	

(Continued)

Jobs Requiring Additional Training Beyond High School

Job Title	How Job Involves Management
A.	
B.	

Jobs Requiring a College Degree or More

Job Title	How Job Involves Management
A.	
B.	

Finding a Job

Application Letter

Name _____

Date _____ **Period** _____

Look through the classified ad section of a newspaper and find a job that interests you. Then write a letter of application as if you were applying for the job. Attach the ad and letter to this page.

Resume Development

Name _____

Date _____ Period _____

Develop your own chronological resume by filling in the information requested below. Then prepare your final resume on another sheet of paper.

Name: _____

Address: _____

Telephone number: _____

Job Objective:

_____

_____

Education:

_____

_____

_____

_____

Work Experience:

_____

_____

_____

_____

Honors and Activities:

_____

_____

_____

_____

Hobbies and Interests:

_____

_____

_____

_____

References:

_____

_____

_____

_____

Traits Leading to Job Success

Name _____

Date _____ **Period** _____

Identify three traits related to job success that you would like to develop or improve in yourself. Then list some steps you might take to improve in each area.

1. Trait: _____

Plans for improvement: _____

_____

_____

_____

_____

_____

_____

_____

_____

2. Trait: _____

Plans for improvement: _____

_____

_____

_____

_____

_____

_____

_____

_____

3. Trait: _____

Plans for improvement: _____

_____

_____

_____

_____

_____

_____

_____

_____

_____

Personal Traits and Job Success

Activity D

Chapter 32

Name _____

Date _____ Period _____

Several traits that can lead to job success are listed below. Explain what each of these traits means and why people who have these traits are likely to be successful at their jobs.

1. Positive attitude: _____

_____

_____

_____

_____

_____

2. Capability: _____

_____

_____

_____

_____

_____

3. Initiative: _____

_____

_____

_____

_____

_____

4. Honesty: _____

_____

_____

_____

_____

_____

5. Dependability: _____

_____

_____

_____

_____

_____